THE STORY OF ABRAHAM LINCOLN

A Biography Book for New Readers

Written by
CARLA JABLONSKI

Illustrated by
PATRICK CORRIGAN

ROCKRIDGE PRESS

For all the people who continue to fight for the rights of others.

And for my father. He would have loved that I wrote this book about one of his heroes.

For general information on our other products and services or to obtain technical support, please contact our Customer Care Department within the United States at (866) 744-2665, or outside the United States at (510) 253-0500.

Rockridge Press publishes its books in a variety of electronic and print formats. Some content that appears in print may not be available in electronic books, and vice versa.

Series Designer: Angela Navarra

Cover and Interior Designer: Jane Archer

Art Producer: Hillary Frileck   Editors: Jeanine Le Ny and Eliza Kirby

Production Editor: Nora Milman

Illustrations © Patrick Corrigan, 2019
Map Illustrations: Creative Market/Mia Buono, pp.7, 10, 17, 29, 33, 45, 54

ISBN: Print 978-1-64611-119-0 | eBook 978-1-64611-120-6

Ro

Printed in China

CONTENTS

CHAPTER 1

A LEADER IS BORN

★ Meet Abraham Lincoln ★

You have probably heard of Abraham Lincoln. He was the 16th president of the United States of America. His face is on both the penny *and* the five-dollar bill. There's a big statue of him in Washington, DC—the Lincoln Memorial. Many people say he was the best president the United States has ever had. That's because without Abraham Lincoln there might not even *be* a United States!

When Abraham Lincoln was president, many people did not agree with one another. The biggest argument was about **slavery**. In some states, it was legal to enslave people and force them to work. The enslaved people were mostly African or African American. By law they were considered property, not people with rights. Their children were enslaved, too. They were bought and sold, forced to work hard, and often treated cruelly. By the time Abraham Lincoln was born, this type of slavery had been part of American life for almost 200 years. When he became president, the argument about slavery would almost tear the United States apart.

From a young age, Abraham knew that slavery was wrong. He loved that America began with the ideas of equality, freedom, and **unity**. As an adult, his brave decisions would help lead to **civil war** and end slavery. So, what led him to become such an amazing president? Let's journey back in time to find out!

> "If slavery is not wrong, nothing is wrong. I cannot remember when I did not so think and feel."

★ Abraham's America ★

Abraham Lincoln was born in Kentucky on February 12, 1809. His family lived in a log cabin with only one room. At night Abraham likely heard wild animals outside in the darkness. Sometimes he and his older sister, Sarah, had to shoo mice out of their corn-husk mattresses so they could sleep. Back then there was no indoor bathroom. They had no running water for washing or cooking. For Abraham's poor family, there wasn't even a wooden floor. It was made of dirt!

JUMP IN THE THINK TANK

What do you think it would be like to live without electricity?

Abraham's parents, Thomas and Nancy, worked hard on their farm. They did not enslave people like the wealthy **plantation** owners. They did their own work. Abraham and Sarah helped, too. Nancy made the clothes for the family. Abraham grew so quickly that sometimes his pants stopped inches above his ankles and his wrists stuck out of his shirts.

If Abraham had time to play, he climbed trees or swam in creeks. Though Nancy couldn't read, she told her family Bible stories from memory by candlelight in the evenings. No one had electricity in their homes then, even in the few small cities.

America was still a new country. When Abraham was born, there were only 17 states.

The rest were called **territories**. Many of the territories wanted to join the **Union**. Some people wanted to keep out any territory that allowed slavery. Others wanted to let each state make its own rules.

Abraham's parents believed no one should be allowed to buy and sell another person. They joined an antislavery church where Abraham listened to sermons about freeing the enslaved people. He didn't know then that these early lessons would one day lead him to change the country forever, and cement his place in history.

WHEN?

The first enslaved people are brought to America

1619

George Washington becomes the first president of the USA

1789

Thomas Lincoln and Nancy Hanks get married

1806

Abraham's sister, Sarah, is born

1807

People can no longer be brought from Africa to be enslaved in the US

1807

Abraham Lincoln is born

1809

CHAPTER 2
THE EARLY YEARS

★ Hard Times ★

When Abraham was seven years old, the Lincoln family moved to Indiana hoping to find better land to farm. When they arrived, they had to cut down trees to build their house. They plowed the fields so they could plant vegetables. Abraham helped with these jobs even though he was very young.

JUMP IN THE THINK TANK

Can you imagine building your family's house from scratch?

Then something terrible happened. Abraham's mother became sick from drinking bad milk, and then later died. Abraham was only nine years old and Sarah was 11 when their mother was laid to rest. Abraham was devastated. He would sit in the corner, reciting Bible stories his mother had told him, as if saying her words made him feel better. But throughout all of Abraham's life, people noticed a sadness in him.

It was hard for Thomas to take care of his children *and* the farm. He decided he needed a new wife. He went back to Kentucky, leaving Abraham and Sarah at home. Abraham was scared. How would they take care of themselves? An older cousin moved in to help, but by the time their father had returned, they were all dirty and hungry. Luckily, their father's new wife quickly changed things—especially for Abraham.

★ Always Learning ★

Abraham loved his stepmother immediately. Sarah Bush Johnston was sweet and kind. She and Thomas had known each other when they were young. Now she was a widow with three children joining her on the farm—John, Elizabeth, and Matilda—but she treated Abraham and Sarah as her own.

Abraham's stepmother made things nicer for everyone. She asked Thomas to put in a real floor. The cabin became much homier—and cleaner. Best of all, she wanted Abraham to learn.

Like Nancy, Sarah couldn't read or write. But both women thought education was important. When Abraham was six, he and his sister had gone to a **one-room schoolhouse** for a few weeks. There he'd learned the alphabet and how to count.

The new Mrs. Lincoln also sent Abraham and Sarah to school. They couldn't go often because they had to help on the farm. Abraham once said he went to school "by littles" because he went just *a little* at a time. All the days he attended school would add up to less than a year. He always wished he could have had more schooling. He worked hard on his own, though. He copied sections from books to practice writing, and then memorized them. Paper was hard to get, so when he ran out he'd write on boards.

Reading opened up whole worlds for Abraham. Once he started, he never wanted to stop. His father sometimes found Abraham reading in the field. Thomas would angrily send Abraham back to work. Thomas couldn't read and saw no need for it. He thought Abraham was lazy. But Abraham loved reading more than farmwork. Abraham and his father grew further and further apart.

> "My best friend is a person who will give me a book I have not read."

Sarah understood Abraham better than his father. She took his side in their many arguments. She even gave Abraham books. Two of his favorites were *Aesop's Fables* and a **biography** of George Washington, the first president of the United States of America. Many of the books included lessons on right and wrong, lessons he'd carry with him for years to come.

WHEN?

Lincoln's family moves to Indiana	Lincoln's mother, Nancy, dies	Thomas Lincoln marries Sarah Bush Johnston
1816	**1818**	**1819**

CHAPTER 3
MAKING HIS MARK

★ Honest Abe ★

By the time Abraham was 16, he was six feet tall and strong. Later, he'd grow to be as tall as six foot four. He was so good with an axe people called him "The Rail Splitter." His father had him work for their neighbors chopping down trees and building fences. Abraham didn't like giving his father the money he earned for his hard work. Abraham wasn't sure what he would be when he grew up, but he knew it *wasn't* going to be a farmer. **Frontier** life didn't suit Abraham. He disliked hunting, which was how his family put food on the table. He once shot a turkey and was so upset about killing a living creature he swore he'd never do it again. When older kids cruelly used turtles in a game, he lectured them. He wanted to work with his *mind,* not just with his hands.

In 1831, a man named Denton Offutt hired Abraham to bring a boat from Illinois down south to New Orleans. This was his second trip down the river. In New Orleans, Abraham was horrified by the sight of enslaved people wearing chains and being whipped. The cruelty sickened him. How could human beings be sold at market, as if they were cattle? He never forgot the experience. "That sight was a continual torment to me," he said.

After the successful trip, Mr. Offutt offered him a job in his store in New Salem, Illinois. Abraham jumped at the chance. He was 22 years old and ready to leave the family farm.

While working at the store, Abraham got to know everyone in New Salem. They enjoyed his funny stories. Abraham had a hearty laugh, and he liked making others laugh, too. He was also known for his honesty. If Abraham made a mistake, he admitted it. If he gave someone the wrong amount of change or tea, he'd make sure to fix it. Because Abraham could read, he helped others who couldn't. Neighbors brought him their mail and important papers. Everyone liked Abraham. Well, *almost* everyone.

★ Respected Abe ★

A gang in New Salem known as the Clary's Grove Boys often picked on newcomers. Their leader, Jack Armstrong, challenged Abraham to a fight. Abraham didn't like to fight, but felt

JUMP IN THE THINK TANK

Do you have ideas about what your government might do to help people now?

he had to do it. Otherwise, people would think he was a coward.

Some said Jack won the fight. Others said Abraham did. But everyone agreed Abraham's strength and courage earned the gang's respect.

After Mr. Offutt's store closed down, Abraham wondered what he should do next. He believed he had good ideas to improve Illinois. He thought there should be more roads and that the rivers should be cleaned up to make traveling easier. The best way to make this happen would be if *he* was part of the government. He decided he'd try to be elected to the **State Assembly**.

The Clary's Grove Boys helped Abraham in the 1832 election. He lost, but he was happy to learn that almost everyone in New Salem voted for him.

The next year, Abraham opened his own store with a partner, William Berry. But business was tough and this store failed. They owed a lot of money. It took many years, but Abraham paid off his share *and* his partner's, who had died. This is when Abraham got the nickname "Honest Abe."

> "Resolve to **be honest** at all events."

If farming life had taught him one thing, it was to work hard and to keep going even after a failure. In 1834, he tried to become a state **legislator** again. This time he won!

WHEN?

1831 — Abraham moves to New Salem, Illinois

1832 — Abraham loses the election for state legislator

1833 — Abraham buys a store with his partner, William Berry

1834 — Abraham is elected to the Illinois House of Representatives

CHAPTER 4

NEVER GIVE UP

★ Springfield and Beyond ★

Abraham borrowed money from a friend to buy his first suit. He wore it to begin his **term** as a legislator. He was 25 years old.

While serving, Abraham watched what the more experienced men did. Many were lawyers. Abraham realized if he became a lawyer, too, he'd be a better **representative** for the people who voted for him. He taught himself enough to earn his law license.

Abraham was elected to a second term and moved to the bigger town of Springfield, which was the new capital of Illinois. He had helped make this change happen! This made him more confident, as did the respect of his fellow legislators. This new confidence also helped Abraham socially. He had always been shy around girls. One day at a party, Abraham walked up to a girl named Mary Todd and asked her to dance. Soon after, they started **courting**.

Some people thought they were an odd couple. Mary's family was rich, and she was well educated. Abraham came from a poor family, and he had barely gone to school. But they both loved poetry and discussing important issues, and they were both against slavery. Mary's relatives, who owned slaves themselves, didn't like Abraham. But Mary married him in 1842 anyway. They would go on to have four sons: Robert; Edward, who died when he was little; William; and Thomas.

The legislature only met for a few months each year, so after he and Mary Todd were married, Abraham also became a circuit lawyer. Circuit lawyers traveled from town to town to argue cases. Abraham needed to bring a lot of paperwork with him. He started carrying his paperwork in his stovepipe hat so he wouldn't lose it. He sometimes still lost important papers, but the tall hat became his trademark.

JUMP IN THE THINK TANK

Abraham taught himself because he couldn't go to school. If you couldn't go to school, what subject would you study hard to learn on your own? Have you ever learned something new on your own? How did it feel?

Abraham worked hard for the people of Illinois. Now he wanted to have a say in the laws for the *whole* country. To do that, he would have to become a member of **Congress**. He didn't win a nomination in 1843, so he couldn't run for the office. Once again, he didn't give up. In 1846 he not only got the nomination to be the candidate, he won the election! He moved to Washington, DC.

After two years in Congress, Abraham felt he wasn't getting anything done. He missed Mary and their sons, who were living with her family in Kentucky. He decided to go back to being a lawyer rather than run for reelection. Mary and the boys joined him again in Springfield.

★ Slavery Must End ★

In 1854, Congress passed a new law called the Kansas-Nebraska Act. It allowed slavery to occur in new states—even if they were in the North. Until then, the law had said the exact opposite—that no states could join the Union with slavery if they were north of Missouri. When Abraham heard about the law, he was "thunderstruck and stunned."

After spending the past six years as a lawyer, Abraham felt he had to get back into government to stop slavery from spreading to the North. He ran for senator against Stephen A. Douglas, the man who'd created the new law. Stephen was Abraham's old rival from the Illinois legislature. He had also once wanted to marry Mary!

> "Whenever I hear **anyone arguing** for slavery, I feel a **strong impulse** to see it tried on him **personally**."

Abraham made a speech against slavery that became famous. He said, "A house divided against itself cannot stand." He meant the

country couldn't be strong if it was split between free states and slave states. It had to be one or the other. It was clear that he believed all states should be free states.

Abraham and Stephen **debated** all over Illinois. Newspapers printed their speeches. People traveled far to hear them.

Abraham didn't win the election, but now he was known beyond Illinois. He was invited to talk in New York City. His speech there convinced people he should run for president.

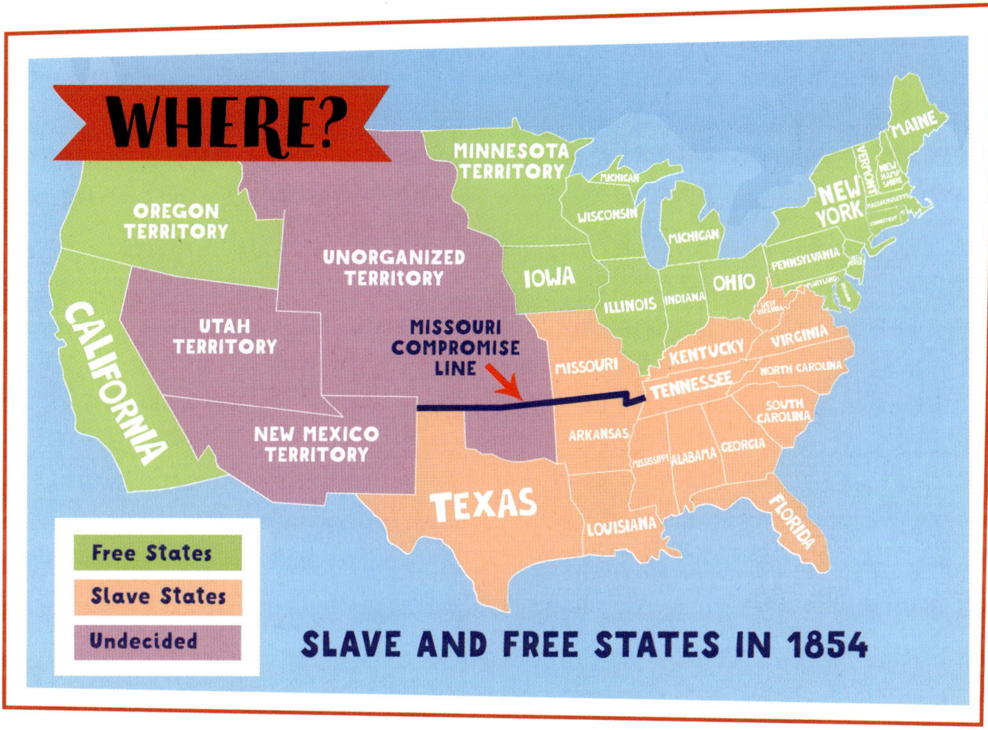

Abraham didn't know if he could win. Several elections hadn't gone his way. More experienced men, including Stephen A. Douglas, were running for president, too. He knew some people thought his stand against slavery was too strong and others felt it wasn't strong enough. But Mary believed in him.

Abraham ran for president but didn't spend much time campaigning. His many supporters campaigned for him, though. They let everyone know how Abraham came from a humble background, and that he had worked hard all his life. During the campaign, a young girl named Grace Bedell suggested in a letter that he grow a beard to look more like a president. Abraham wrote back in good humor, not making any promises. In the end, the votes were split among several candidates. Abraham won the most votes of all—though none from the southern states.

On November 6, 1860, Abraham was elected the 16th president of the United States. A few days later, he decided to grow a beard.

WHEN?

1854	1858	1858	1860
Kansas-Nebraska Act is approved	Abraham gives "House Divided" speech	Abraham loses election to Stephen A. Douglas	Abraham is elected the 16th president

CHAPTER 5
PRESIDENT LINCOLN

★ Civil War ★

Southern slaveholders hated that Abraham won the election. They believed he was going to free the enslaved people, making it harder to run their farms. Abraham wasn't officially president yet when seven slave states **seceded** from the Union. Alabama, Florida, Georgia, Louisiana, Mississippi, South Carolina, and Texas declared they were their own country. They elected their own president, Jefferson Davis. They had their own flag and called themselves the Confederate States of America. To Abraham and the northern states, they were rebels.

People in the North disagreed about what to do. Let the states secede? Go to war? Allow them to continue slavery so they wouldn't secede?

As president, it was Abraham's duty to uphold the law. He believed separating from the Union was against the **United States Constitution**.

But in the southern states, slavery was also the law. Abraham hoped he could reason with the southern states to end it.

At his **inauguration**, Abraham warned that he wouldn't allow the country to be split in two. He also made it clear he didn't want to go to war. "We must not be enemies," he said.

Then a problem at Fort Sumter in South Carolina changed everything. The soldiers at the fort were loyal to Abraham and the northern Union, even though the fort was in the Confederate South. The Confederates tried to make the soldiers leave. They wouldn't.

Abraham sent help. He hoped when South Carolina saw he wasn't going to back down, they would return to the Union. Instead, Confederate soldiers shot at the men delivering supplies to the fort. Abraham couldn't avoid war any longer. Those shots started the Civil War.

Abraham had many **volunteers** to fight. Very few had training. Abraham wasn't experienced, either. He had been in the **militia** years earlier

> "As a nation we began by declaring that 'All men are created equal.' We now practically read it 'All men are created equal, except negroes.'"

MYTH & FACT

MYTH: Abraham fought the Civil War to end slavery.

FACT: He did think slavery was wrong. But his biggest reason for going to war was to hold the country together. He believed he needed to show that states couldn't just stop being part of the Union if they didn't like a law.

but he'd never gone to battle. He joked that the only fighting he did was against mosquitoes!

Abraham had to learn to take charge of armies. He read books about **military strategy** and spoke to commanders. Once again, he was determined to teach himself what he needed to know.

★ Inside the White House ★

When the Civil War began, Mary Todd Lincoln had just moved into the **White House** with her husband a month earlier. Mary was excited that

JUMP IN THE THINK TANK

What would it be like if one of your parents were president?

Abraham was elected president. She was pleased to be married to such an important man. She quickly went to work decorating the White House, which had become run-down over the years. Their oldest son, Robert, was away at college, but Willie and Tad loved their new home. There was so much space to run around—inside and out.

Abraham didn't change his ways as president. He was still kind and told folksy tales to make his points. He met with anyone who wanted to see him and gave great advice, earning him the love of the people and the nickname "Father Abraham."

The war was a terrible burden for him. He hated any loss of life. In battle after battle, thousands of soldiers died, and the Union seemed to be losing. No wonder he welcomed Tad and

Willie into his office whenever they wanted. They were allowed to interrupt his meetings and play with their toy soldiers while he and his generals discussed the war. The boys lifted his dark moods. "If I did not laugh, I should die," he said.

As the war continued, Abraham and Mary sometimes argued. He wanted her to stop spending so much money—he needed it for his army! They were both upset when gossip spread that Mary was a spy. Abraham wasn't surprised. She was from a southern family that practiced slavery. But he knew Mary went against her own family. She agreed with Abraham about slavery and the importance of keeping the Union together.

Then tragedy hit the White House. In February 1862, Willie fell sick and died. Abraham burst into tears when he told his assistant the terrible news. But he had no time to dwell on his sadness. There was so much he had to do as president.

WHEN?

Abraham elected president

NOVEMBER 6, **1860**

South Carolina secedes

DECEMBER **1860**

Mississippi. Florida, Alabama, Georgia, and Louisiana secede

JANUARY **1861**

Texas secedes

FEBRUARY **1861**

Abraham inaugurated as president of the United States

MARCH 4, **1861**

WHEN?

Shots fired at Fort Sumter; the Civil War begins

APRIL 12, **1861**

Virginia secedes

APRIL **1861**

Arkansas and North Carolina secede

MAY **1861**

Tennessee secedes

JUNE **1861**

William Wallace Lincoln dies at age 11

FEBRUARY 20, **1862**

CHAPTER 6

ALL MEN ARE CREATED EQUAL

JUMP IN THE THINK TANK

If you had to make a hard decision, what might help you make it?

Emancipation Proclamation

Everyone had believed the Civil War would end quickly, but it dragged on and on. Abraham sadly visited battlefields and hospitals. The number of dead rose to the thousands, and the Union Army had been losing most of the battles. Many people in the North thought Abraham was making mistakes.

Abraham struggled with what to do. He was getting pressure from all sides. Some argued he had to free the enslaved people right away. But, Abraham worried, would that make even *more* states secede?

Others simply wanted peace. They suggested Abraham give in to the South. But that was like giving in to a bully. He knew he had to win the war to bring the South back into the Union. But how?

The first thing he did was to change his generals. Abraham was frustrated with General George McClellan. McClellan often retreated when Abraham thought he should press forward. Eventually, Abraham was tired of McClellan's excuses. He replaced him with General Ambrose Burnside. Other important additions who helped bring victories for the Union were Generals William T. Sherman and Ulysses S. Grant.

Then Abraham realized he could use laws about slavery *against* the Confederate states. The president was allowed to take an enemy's property if it was being used to fight against the country. Slaveholders considered enslaved people to be their property. They were forcing these people to help them in the war. This gave Abraham the ability to take them away.

> I have a **right** to take any measure which may best **subdue** the enemy.

But he wasn't actually going to *take* the people away. He was going to *free* them.

On January 1, 1863, Abraham announced the **Emancipation Proclamation**. From that day on, any enslaved person living in the Confederate states was free. The freed people could join the Union Army. Almost 200,000 black men signed up. This gave the Union the additional soldiers

they needed, and it took away a major resource from the South.

★ Gettysburg Address ★

Meanwhile, General Robert E. Lee of the Confederate Army was bringing his troops farther and farther north. In the summer of 1863, the Union troops met them in Gettysburg, Pennsylvania, where they fought a big battle. The

Confederate Army was defeated, and they retreated back south. They never came that far north again. It was a turning point in the war.

Gettysburg was one of the bloodiest battles of the war. A portion of the battlefield was set aside as a cemetery for the fallen soldiers.

A ceremony was held there on November 19, 1863. Abraham was invited to be one of the speakers at a full day of speeches and music. Others spoke for hours, but Abraham's speech lasted less than three minutes. They were the most important three minutes of his career—and for the future of the country.

He explained to the 15,000 people listening why the war was so important. He believed the war was a test. In 1776, he said, the United States began with the idea that all men are created equal. Would the country that the **founding fathers** created be able to last? "Government of the people, by the people, for the people shall

not **perish** from the earth," he said.

Abraham made people understand that the Union Army was fighting for an *idea*. It was fighting for democracy and a belief in equality.

It was a fight for what kind of country America should be.

WHEN?

Emancipation Proclamation	The Battle of Gettysburg	Abraham delivers the Gettysburg Address
JANUARY 1, **1863**	JULY 1–3, **1863**	NOVEMBER 19, **1863**

CHAPTER 7

ONE NATION ONCE AGAIN

★ Ending Slavery ★

It was time for another election. Many people believed Abraham would lose this one—including Abraham. Everyone was tired of the war. Abraham was, too. He was sad over the loss of so many soldiers. He knew what it was like when loved ones died.

But after the Union won Gettysburg and a few other important battles, it looked as if the war might soon be over. Abraham won the election in a landslide. This big victory reassured Abraham that he was doing the right thing.

The Emancipation Proclamation was a wartime law and only temporary. So Abraham decided to make a *permanent* law and add it to the Constitution. On January 31, 1865, Congress passed the 13th **Amendment**, ending slavery forever. Everything Abraham believed in since he was a child was coming together.

He began to plan what he would do after the war. Many southern cities and farms had been destroyed and needed help. Abraham would aid in the **Reconstruction**. He also wanted to help black and white Americans learn to live together as equals.

> "With malice toward none; with charity toward all . . . let us strive on to finish the work we are in; to bind up the nation's wounds."

On March 4, 1865, Abraham took his second **oath of office** as president. Abraham didn't brag about Union victories or gloat. Instead, he talked about what mattered most to him: finding a way for the country to be whole again once the war was finally over.

★ Lincoln's Last Day ★

Not everyone at the inauguration was celebrating. A man named John Wilkes Booth was a famous actor who believed in slavery and was against the Union. He was furious that Abraham had been reelected president. He hated Abraham, blaming him for all the losses of life and property in the South. He also feared—quite rightly— that Abraham would give the newly freed

JUMP IN THE THINK TANK

What would be the first thing you would have done to bring the North and South together again?

MYTH & FACT

MYTH: Abraham Lincoln was the first president to make Thanksgiving a national holiday.

FACT: Thanksgiving had been celebrated to give thanks for the harvest before, but Abraham made it a federal holiday to celebrate the survival of the nation after the Civil War.

people more legal rights, including the right to vote. Booth didn't want that to happen. He didn't think they were the equals of white people.

On April 14, 1865, Abraham and Mary went to the theater with their guests Major Henry Rathbone and Clara Harris. The long war and the death of Willie had taken their toll on the Lincoln family. Abraham looked older. He and Mary sometimes lost their tempers. Abraham told Mary, "We must both be more cheerful in the future." Having a night out seemed like a good way to start.

The whole city knew the Lincolns were going to the show. Because Booth was an actor, he had no trouble getting inside. He snuck up behind Abraham and shot him once in the head. Then he leapt down to the stage from the balcony, shouting, "The South is avenged!"

Abraham was carried to a nearby boardinghouse. A doctor raced over to help but there was nothing to be done. Abraham Lincoln died the next morning.

People cried in the streets. Flags hung at half-mast and buildings were covered in black fabric. Mary was so upset she couldn't attend Abraham's funeral. Everyone understood.

Abraham's coffin was put on a train to bring him to Springfield, Illinois, where he would be buried. His son Willie's coffin was removed from the nearby cemetery and put on the train, too.

The train stopped in 10 cities so that thousands of people could pay their respects. The train arrived in Springfield on May 3, 1865. Willie and Abraham were laid to rest side by side in the Oak Ridge Cemetery.

Abraham never had the chance to see Congress pass the 14th and 15th Amendments that gave the people he freed full citizenship and the right to vote. He wouldn't be able to help the country mend its wounds from the war. But he had put it all into motion. His hopes for the country continued on. It continues on whenever people fight for the rights of others.

WHEN?

Abraham reelected as president

NOVEMBER 8,
1864

13th Amendment passed by Congress abolishing slavery

JANUARY 31,
1865

Abraham inaugurated for second term as president

MARCH 4,
1865

General Lee surrenders to General Grant, ending the Civil War

APRIL 9,
1865

Abraham **assassinated**

APRIL 14,
1865

CHAPTER 8

SO . . . WHO WAS ABRAHAM LINCOLN?

★ Challenge Accepted! ★

You have learned a lot about Abraham Lincoln! Let's see what you can remember!

1 What is Abraham most remembered for?

→ A Being an excellent hunter
→ B Winning every election he ever ran in
→ C Making straight A's in law school
→ D Ending slavery

2 When was Abraham born?

→ A 1776
→ B 1809
→ C 1865
→ D 1900

3 Where was Abraham born?

→ A Indiana
→ B New York
→ C Illinois
→ D Kentucky

4 **What kind of house did Abraham live in when he was a child?**

→ A A brick house

→ B A log cabin

→ C A mansion

→ D A tent

5 **What was Abraham's favorite thing to do as a kid?**

→ A Read

→ B Chop down trees

→ C Hunt

→ D Watch TV

6 **Abraham was elected to be *which* number president of the United States?**

→ A the 1st

→ B the 5th

→ C the 16th

→ D the 20th

7 **When Abraham was elected, war broke out. What was that war called?**

→ A The American Revolution

→ B The War of the Roses

→ C The War of the Worlds

→ D The Civil War

8 Which was NOT one of Abraham's nicknames?

→ A Honest Abe
→ B The Rail Splitter
→ C Father Abraham
→ D The Tall Boy

9 What did the states that seceded call themselves?

→ A The Fighting States
→ B The True United States
→ C The Confederate States of America
→ D The Union of the South

10 Abraham introduced a law during the war that freed enslaved people in the southern states. What was that law called?

→ A The Emancipation Proclamation
→ B The Freedom Act
→ C The Equality Amendment
→ D The 20th Amendment

11. Which amendment *permanently* ended slavery?

→ A The 1st Amendment
→ B The 7th Amendment
→ C The 13th Amendment
→ D The 19th Amendment

12. **Who assassinated President Abraham Lincoln?**

- A John Wilkes Booth
- B General Robert E. Lee
- C Stephen A. Douglas
- D Jack Armstrong

13. **Where was Abraham Lincoln when he was shot?**

- A At a parade
- B On a train
- C At a theater
- D At home at the White House

Answers 1. D; 2. B; 3. D; 4. B; 5. A; 6. C; 7. D; 8. D; 9. C; 10. A; 11. C; 12. A; 13. C

★ Our World ★

Many historians believe Abraham Lincoln changed America more than any other president. Let's look at some ways those changes are still having an impact today.

The biggest impact Abraham had on the country was in ending slavery once and for all. In his speeches, he reminded everyone that the United States was founded on the idea of all men being created equal. That equality didn't come easily. Not everyone was ready to accept non-white Americans—or women—as true equals. For many years, dedicated and brave people fought—and continue to fight—to bring Abraham's vision of equality to life. The civil rights movement of the 1950s and 1960s came into existence to make sure African Americans had the rights promised in the Constitution. There have also been groups working for the rights of women since Abraham's time. Unfortunately, people's rights are still sometimes ignored. Courageous people continue to work hard to make sure that Abraham's belief in a country where *all* people are equal doesn't "perish from this earth."

It has been said that Abraham's life story helped to create the idea of "The American Dream." This is the belief that no matter what your background might be, you could still grow up to become whatever you want. Even president! Two recent presidents who came from humble beginnings are the 42nd president, President Clinton (1993–2001) and the 44th president, President Obama (2009–2017). In fact, without Abraham Lincoln, Barack Obama might never have been elected president. He was the first African American to rise to that office. President Obama even had Abraham Lincoln's own Bible at his inauguration.

Abraham was determined to hold the Union together. He made the world see that a state couldn't simply decide to stop being part of the United States. As a result, the country has grown from the original 13 colonies to 50 states. The United States has become a powerful and wealthy democracy.

Abraham's influence went far beyond the United States. He has been a hero around the world to anyone fighting for equal rights. His face has been on stamps in 100 countries!

JUMP IN THE THINK TANK FOR MORE!

→ The 15th Amendment passed in 1870 granted the right to vote to African American men. Women—black or white—were still not allowed. Women worked 50 more years to have the same right, sometimes facing violence. Why is being able to vote so important?

→ Abraham listened to many different points of view. He even hired people he disagreed with as his advisors. How might it be useful to hear from people who don't agree with you?

→ The United States is still a single country because Abraham was determined to hold the Union together. What might it be like today if the states that seceded had never rejoined?

→ The idea that everyone in the United States is equal is written into the Constitution and something Abraham believed in deeply. But even after the Civil War, people have not always been treated as equals. Can you think of any examples?

Glossary

amendment: An addition or change to the United States Constitution

assassinate: To kill an important person

biography: A person's life story

civil war: A war between people in the same country

Congress: The branch of the US government that makes laws

courting: An old-fashioned word for dating

debate: An argument on a specific topic

emancipation: Being freed

founding fathers: The men who wrote the United States Constitution to create the United States of America. Well-known examples are John Adams, Benjamin Franklin, Alexander Hamilton, John Jay, Thomas Jefferson, James Madison, and George Washington.

frontier: The area that is at the very edge of settled lands

inauguration: The ceremony to mark the beginning of something, such as the beginning of Abraham Lincoln's presidency

legislator: A person who makes laws

military strategy: The planning for an army

militia: A group of citizens who fight as soldiers in an emergency

oath of office: A solemn promise to do the right thing in one's job

one-room schoolhouse: A school where children of all ages and grades are taught by a teacher in a single room

perish: To die

plantation: A very large farm growing crops for sale

proclamation: An official announcement

reconstruction: Rebuilding something damaged or broken

representative: A person elected to speak for the people who voted for him or her

secede: To officially withdraw

slavery: A system in which people are treated like property and forced to work for no wages

State Assembly: The governmental organization in many states that helps to make laws for that state

term: A specific length of time

territories: Areas of land that weren't states yet

Union: The northern states that stayed together after southern states seceded

United States Constitution: The document that lays out the laws and rights of the United States, which was finished and signed in 1787

unity: Being joined together

volunteer: A person who decides to join something without being asked

White House: The place where United States presidents live

Bibliography

Abraham Lincoln on Encyclopedia Britannica (https://www.britannica.com/biography/Abraham-Lincoln)

Abraham Lincoln Online (http://www.abrahamlincolnonline.org/lincoln.html)

Abraham Lincoln's Childhood: Growing Up to Be President (https://americacomesalive.com/2013/02/12/abraham-lincoln-1809-1865-president-from-1861-1865)

Abraham Lincoln: Life Before the Presidency (https://millercenter.org/president/lincoln/life-before-the-presidency)

Abraham Lincoln's Thoughts on Slavery (https://www.nps.gov/libo/learn/historyculture/thoughts-on-slavery.htm)

Benoit, Peter. *Abraham Lincoln*, A True Book. New York: Scholastic, 2012.

Benoit, Peter. *Abraham Lincoln*, Cornerstones of Freedom. New York: Scholastic, 2012.

Blashfield, Jean F. *Slavery in America*, A True Book. New York: Scholastic, 2012.

The Collected Works of Abraham Lincoln (https://quod.lib.umich.edu/l/lincoln)

Dussling Jennifer. *Long, Tall Lincoln*. New York: Harper, 2017.

The Emancipation Proclamation (https://www.archives.gov/exhibits/featured-documents/emancipation-proclamation)

Gilpin, Caroline Crosson. *Abraham Lincoln*. Washington, DC: National Geographic Society, 2012.

Kanefield, Teri. *Abraham Lincoln, The Making of America*. New York: Abrams Books, 2018.

Keneally, Thomas. *Abraham Lincoln: A Life*, Penguin Lives. New York: Viking, 2003.

Kimmel, Allison Crotzer. *Slavery in the United States*, Primary Source History. North Mankato, MN: Capstone Press, 2015.

Lincoln's Assassination (https://www.fords.org/lincolns-assassination)

Lincoln's Homes (https://www.nps.gov/liho/learn/historyculture/lhomes.htm)

McPherson, James M. *Abraham Lincoln*. New York: Oxford University Press, 2009.

Pascal, Janet B. *Who Was Abraham Lincoln?* New York: Grosset & Dunlap, 2008.

Rappaport, Doreen. *Abe's Honest Words: The Life of Abraham Lincoln*, Big Words. New York: Hyperion Books for Children, 2008.

Stone, Tanya Lee. *Abraham Lincoln*. New York: DK Publishing, 2005.

Under His Hat (http://underhishat.alplm.org/intheclassroom.html)

About the Author

Carla Jablonski is the author and editor of dozens of books for middle-grade and young adult readers. Her middle-grade graphic novel trilogy, *Resistance* (First Second Books), about children in the French Resistance during World War II, won a Sydney Taylor Award. She provided research and editorial direction for the award-winning middle-grade historical fiction series Turning Points (Aladdin Books). She often writes for Disney Press, and is also the author of two books in the Parragon biography series STEM Stars, about women in science and technology. In addition to being a writer, Jablonski is an actor, singer, and aerialist. She also teaches workshops for the Alan Alda Center for Communicating Science, helping scientists at all stages of their careers improve how they talk about their work to audiences of all ages and experience levels.

About the Illustrator

Patrick Corrigan was born on a crisp, cold December day in a small, cloudy town in Cheshire, England. With a passion for precision as a child, he grew up patiently drawing and designing arts and crafts.

This took him to study ceramics at university, train as an art teacher, and eventually become an art director at a busy design studio where he worked for nearly 10 years. While there he honed his skills working on well over 500 educational and picture books for children as well as animations and branding.

Now based in Hammersmith, West London—where he lives with his newspaper editor wife, Dulcie, and their fat cat Forbes—Patrick uses Photoshop, Illustrator, and sometimes even real art equipment to create his work. He draws best when listening to his vast collection of vinyl that he often hides from his wife.